Unmasking Narcissistic Personality Disorder

Strategies for Dealing with Narcissists in Personal and Professional Relationships

BY
Margot Pearson

Table of Content

Introduction..**7**

Chapter 1...**13**

Understanding Narcissistic Personality Disorder............. **13**

Definition of NPD.. 13

Types of Narcissism..15

Prevalence and Statistics... 18

Common Misconceptions..20

Chapter 2...**25**

The Roots of Narcissism.. **25**

Psychological Theories and Causes.............................25

   Psychoanalytic Theories..................................... 25

   Behavioral Theories... 26

   Cognitive Theories...27

Childhood Influences and Family Dynamics.................. 28

   Parental Influence.. 28

   Early Life Experiences..29

   Family Dynamics... 29

Genetic and Environmental Factors.............................. 30

   Genetic Factors... 30

   Environmental Factors.. 30

Chapter 3...**33**

Identifying Narcissistic Behaviors.............................. **33**

Common Traits and Behaviors..................................... 33

      1. Grandiose Sense of Self-Importance....... 33

      2. Preoccupation with Fantasies...................34

      3. Belief in Being Special and Unique.........34

4. Need for Excessive Admiration............35

5. Sense of Entitlement............35

6. Interpersonal Exploitativeness............35

7. Lack of Empathy............36

8. Envy and Belief That Others Are Envious of Them............36

9. Arrogant and Haughty Behaviors............36

Identifying Signs and Red Flags............37

Red Flag 1: Constant Need for Attention and Admiration............37

Red Flag 2: Exploitative Relationships............37

Red Flag 3: Lack of Genuine Empathy............38

Red Flag 4: Unrealistic Expectations and Entitlement............38

Red Flag 5: Envy and Competitiveness............38

Narcissistic Communication Styles............39

Dominance and Control............39

Manipulation and Deception............40

Lack of Empathy............40

Arrogance and Condescension............41

Charm and Charisma............41

Case Studies............41

Case Study 1: The Charismatic CEO............41

Case Study 2: The Overbearing Parent............42

Case Study 3: The Charming Partner............43

Chapter 4............**45**

Impact of Narcissism on Relationships............**45**

Personal Relationships............45

Effects on Family............45

Effects on Friends...................................... 46

Effects on Romantic Partners.....................47

Professional Relationships...............................48

Impact in the Workplace............................. 48

Career Progression.....................................48

Emotional and Psychological Consequences.................. 49

Mental Health Effects................................. 49

Cognitive Effects..50

Behavioral Effects.......................................50

Recovery and Healing.................................50

Chapter 5..**53**

Strategies for Dealing with Narcissists in Personal Relationships...**53**

Setting Boundaries..53

Importance of Setting Boundaries............... 53

Techniques for Setting Boundaries.............. 54

Effective Communication...............................56

Strategies for Assertive Communication..... 57

Self-Care and Support.................................... 59

Maintaining Personal Well-Being................ 60

Building a Support Network........................ 61

When to Walk Away.. 63

Signs It's Time to End the Relationship.......63

Steps to Ending the Relationship................. 65

Chapter 6..**69**

Strategies for Dealing with Narcissists in Professional Relationships...**69**

Managing Expectations.................................. 69

Realistic Expectations in the Workplace......69

Conflict Resolution..71

    Techniques for Resolving Conflicts............71

Building a Support Network.............................74

    Seeking Support from Colleagues and
Mentors... 74

Legal and HR Considerations...........................77

    Knowing Your Rights................................. 77

    When to Involve HR.................................. 78

Chapter 7...**83**

Healing from Narcissistic Abuse.....................**83**

Recognizing Narcissistic Abuse....................... 83

    Identifying Signs of Abuse......................... 83

Steps to Recovery.. 86

    Healing Strategies and Techniques.............. 86

Therapeutic Interventions................................ 89

    Types of Therapy and Their Benefits...........90

Building Resilience...93

    Developing Emotional Strength and
Resilience.. 93

Chapter 8...**99**

Helping Others Understand and Deal with Narcissists.... 99

Educating Loved Ones.....................................99

    Teaching Others About NPD....................... 99

Offering Guidance on Dealing with Narcissists............ 102

    Strategies for Dealing with Narcissists...... 103

Supporting Someone in a Narcissistic Relationship......106

    Providing Help and Guidance.................... 106

Raising Awareness...109

    Advocating for Broader Understanding and

Support...109

Conclusion...113

Introduction

Welcome Message

Welcome to "Unmasking Narcissistic Personality Disorder: Strategies for Dealing with Narcissists in Personal and Professional Relationships." This book is designed to be your guide through the often confusing and painful world of interactions with individuals who have Narcissistic Personality Disorder (NPD). Whether you have a narcissist in your personal life, such as a family member or partner, or you are dealing with one in your professional environment, this book will provide you with the knowledge, tools, and strategies needed to manage these challenging relationships.

Introduction to the Topic and the Importance of Understanding NPD

Narcissistic Personality Disorder is a complex and often misunderstood mental health condition. People with NPD exhibit a pervasive pattern of grandiosity, a constant need for admiration, and a lack of empathy for others. These traits can lead to significant interpersonal problems and emotional distress for those around them. Understanding NPD is crucial because it empowers you to recognize the signs and behaviors associated with this disorder, thus enabling you to protect yourself and make informed decisions about how to interact with narcissists. By gaining insight into the underlying causes and dynamics of NPD, you can navigate these relationships more effectively and maintain your own well-being.

Purpose of the Book

The primary purpose of this book is to demystify Narcissistic Personality Disorder and provide practical strategies for dealing with narcissists in both personal and professional settings. It aims to equip you with a comprehensive understanding of NPD, including its roots, manifestations, and impacts on relationships. Moreover, this book seeks to offer actionable advice on how to manage and mitigate the effects of narcissistic behaviors, ensuring you can maintain healthy boundaries and prioritize your mental and emotional health.

Objectives and Goals for Readers

- **Awareness:** Enhance your awareness and understanding of NPD and its characteristics.
- **Identification:** Equip you with the ability to identify narcissistic behaviors and patterns in individuals.
- **Strategies:** Provide effective strategies for managing relationships with narcissists, both personally and professionally.

- **Recovery:** Offer guidance on healing and recovering from narcissistic abuse.
- **Support:** Help you support others who are dealing with narcissists and raise awareness about NPD in your community.

Overview

This book is structured to take you on a comprehensive journey through understanding and dealing with Narcissistic Personality Disorder. Each chapter builds upon the previous one, ensuring a cohesive and thorough exploration of the topic.

- **Chapter 1: Understanding Narcissistic Personality Disorder**
  - Learn about the clinical criteria, types, and common misconceptions of NPD.
- **Chapter 2: The Roots of Narcissism**
  - Explore the psychological theories, childhood influences, and genetic factors contributing to NPD.
- **Chapter 3: Identifying Narcissistic Behaviors**
  - Discover the common traits and behaviors of narcissists, supported by case studies.
- **Chapter 4: Impact of Narcissism on Relationships**

- o Understand how NPD affects personal and professional relationships, and the emotional consequences.
- **Chapter 5: Strategies for Dealing with Narcissists in Personal Relationships**
  - o Gain practical strategies for setting boundaries, effective communication, and self-care.
- **Chapter 6: Strategies for Dealing with Narcissists in Professional Relationships**
  - o Learn techniques for managing expectations, conflict resolution, and building a support network at work.
- **Chapter 7: Healing from Narcissistic Abuse**
  - o Get guidance on recognizing abuse, steps to recovery, and building resilience.
- **Chapter 8: Helping Others Understand and Deal with Narcissists**
  - o Find out how to educate loved ones, support others, and raise awareness about NPD.

How to Use This Book

To get the most out of this book, I recommend the following tips:

1. **Read Sequentially:** While each chapter can stand alone, reading the book sequentially will

provide a deeper, more cohesive understanding of NPD.

2. **Reflect and Take Notes:** As you read, reflect on your experiences and take notes. This will help you internalize the information and apply it to your own life.

3. **Use the Tools and Exercises:** Throughout the book, you will find practical tools, checklists, and exercises. Engage with these actively to develop your skills in managing relationships with narcissists.

4. **Apply the Strategies:** Don't just read about the strategies—apply them in your daily life. Practice setting boundaries, communicating assertively, and seeking support.

5. **Seek Support if Needed:** If at any point you feel overwhelmed or in need of professional help, don't hesitate to reach out to a mental health professional.

By following these tips, you will be well on your way to understanding and managing the complexities of Narcissistic Personality Disorder, ultimately leading to healthier and more fulfilling relationships.

Chapter 1

Understanding Narcissistic Personality Disorder

Definition of NPD

Narcissistic Personality Disorder (NPD) is a mental health condition characterized by a long-term pattern of exaggerated self-importance, an overwhelming need for admiration, and a lack of empathy for others. People with NPD often believe they are superior to others and have little regard for other people's feelings. However, behind this mask of extreme confidence lies a fragile self-esteem that's vulnerable to the slightest criticism.

Clinical Criteria and Characteristics

According to the Diagnostic and Statistical Manual of Mental Disorders (DSM-5), NPD is diagnosed based on specific clinical criteria. To be diagnosed with NPD, an individual must exhibit at least five of the following nine characteristics:

1. **Grandiose Sense of Self-Importance**: Exaggerating achievements and talents,

expecting to be recognized as superior without commensurate achievements.

2. **Preoccupation with Fantasies of Unlimited Success, Power, Brilliance, Beauty, or Ideal Love**: Engaging in elaborate fantasies about having unlimited power or success.

3. **Belief in Being Special and Unique**: Believing they are special and can only be understood by, or should associate with, other special or high-status people or institutions.

4. **Need for Excessive Admiration**: Requiring constant admiration and recognition from others.

5. **Sense of Entitlement**: Having unreasonable expectations of especially favorable treatment or automatic compliance with their expectations.

6. **Interpersonally Exploitative Behavior**: Taking advantage of others to achieve their own ends.

7. **Lack of Empathy**: Being unwilling or unable to recognize or identify with the feelings and needs of others.

8. **Envy of Others or Belief That Others Are Envious of Them**: Often being envious of others or believing others are envious of them.

9. **Arrogant and Haughty Behaviors or Attitudes**: Displaying arrogant, haughty behaviors or attitudes.

People with NPD often have difficulties in their relationships and may experience significant issues in their personal and professional lives. Their behavior can be off-putting to others, and their lack of empathy and exploitative tendencies can cause considerable emotional harm.

Types of Narcissism

Narcissistic Personality Disorder can manifest in different forms, with the two main types being grandiose narcissism and vulnerable narcissism. Understanding these types can provide deeper insight into the various ways NPD can affect behavior and relationships.

Grandiose Narcissism

Grandiose narcissism is the type most commonly associated with NPD and is characterized by overt expressions of superiority and self-importance. Individuals with grandiose narcissism typically exhibit the following traits:

- **Overconfidence and Arrogance**: They often have an inflated sense of their own abilities and achievements and believe they are superior to others.

- **Dominance and Assertiveness**: They tend to be dominant and assertive, often taking charge in social and professional situations.
- **Seek Attention and Admiration**: They have an insatiable need for attention and admiration from others and may engage in behaviors designed to draw focus to themselves.
- **Lack of Empathy**: They have little regard for the feelings and needs of others and may exploit people to achieve their own goals.
- **Aggressiveness**: They can be aggressive and confrontational, especially when their sense of superiority is challenged.

Individuals with grandiose narcissism often come across as confident and charismatic, but their relationships are usually shallow and self-serving. They may struggle with maintaining long-term relationships due to their exploitative and unempathetic nature.

Vulnerable Narcissism

Vulnerable narcissism, also known as covert narcissism, is less apparent and more subtle than grandiose narcissism. Individuals with vulnerable narcissism may appear shy or introverted, but they still harbor feelings of superiority and entitlement. Key characteristics of vulnerable narcissism include:

- **Hypersensitivity to Criticism**: They are extremely sensitive to criticism and may react defensively or with hostility when they perceive any slight.
- **Insecurity and Fragile Self-Esteem**: Despite outward appearances, they have low self-esteem and an intense fear of rejection or inadequacy.
- **Passive-Aggressive Behavior**: They may express their narcissism through passive-aggressive behaviors rather than overt dominance.
- **Introversion and Social Withdrawal**: They may withdraw from social situations to protect themselves from perceived threats to their self-esteem.
- **Victim Mentality**: They often see themselves as victims and may use their perceived victimhood to manipulate others.

Vulnerable narcissists can be more challenging to identify because their narcissistic traits are not as overt. They may come across as humble or self-effacing, but they still possess a deep need for admiration and validation. Their relationships are often marked by dependency and passive-aggressive behavior, and they may use guilt or manipulation to get their needs met.

Understanding the definition, clinical criteria, and types of Narcissistic Personality Disorder is crucial for recognizing and dealing with narcissistic behaviors in various contexts. Both grandiose and vulnerable narcissists present unique challenges, but with the right knowledge and strategies, it is possible to navigate relationships with individuals who have NPD effectively. In the following chapters, we will explore the roots of narcissism, its impact on relationships, and practical strategies for managing interactions with narcissists in both personal and professional settings.

Prevalence and Statistics

Narcissistic Personality Disorder (NPD) is considered relatively uncommon compared to other personality disorders. However, its impact can be profound on both individuals and those around them.

How Common is NPD?

- **General Population:** Estimates suggest that NPD affects approximately 1% to 6% of the general population. The variation in prevalence rates can be attributed to differences in diagnostic criteria, study methodologies, and population samples.

- **Gender Differences:** NPD is more commonly diagnosed in men than in women. Studies indicate that men are two to three times more likely to be diagnosed with NPD.
- **Age Factors:** Symptoms of NPD typically emerge in early adulthood, though they can manifest during adolescence. The disorder often becomes more pronounced in middle age when personal and professional failures become more apparent.
- **Cultural Considerations:** Cultural factors can influence the expression and recognition of narcissistic traits. Societal norms and values around success, individualism, and self-promotion can impact the prevalence and perception of NPD.

While these statistics provide a general sense of how widespread NPD is, it's important to note that many individuals with narcissistic traits may not meet the full criteria for a formal diagnosis. Moreover, cultural and contextual factors can influence how narcissism is expressed and perceived.

Common Misconceptions

There are several misconceptions about NPD that contribute to misunderstanding and stigma. Distinguishing myths from facts is essential for accurate knowledge and effective management of the disorder.

Myth vs. Fact

Myth 1: Narcissism is just about having high self-esteem.

- **Fact:** While high self-esteem involves a healthy sense of self-worth, narcissism is characterized by an exaggerated sense of self-importance and a need for excessive admiration. Narcissists often have fragile self-esteem that depends on external validation and can be easily threatened by criticism.

Myth 2: All narcissists are extroverted and confident.

- **Fact:** Narcissism can manifest in different forms, including grandiose and vulnerable narcissism. While grandiose narcissists are often extroverted and overtly confident, vulnerable narcissists may appear shy, introverted, and insecure but still harbor a sense of superiority and entitlement.

Myth 3: Narcissists are always easy to identify.

- **Fact:** Narcissists can be difficult to recognize, especially those with vulnerable narcissism. They may present as humble or self-effacing, making their narcissistic traits less apparent. Additionally, narcissists can be charming and charismatic, which can mask their underlying personality disorder.

Myth 4: Narcissists can never change.

- **Fact:** While NPD is a persistent and challenging condition to treat, change is possible with the right interventions. Therapy, particularly approaches like cognitive-behavioral therapy (CBT) and schema therapy, can help individuals with NPD develop healthier behaviors and coping mechanisms. However, the motivation to change often depends on the individual's insight and willingness to engage in therapy.

Myth 5: Narcissists don't have feelings.

- **Fact:** Narcissists do have feelings, but they often struggle with empathy and understanding the emotions of others. They may experience intense emotions, such as anger, envy, and shame, particularly when their self-image is threatened.

Their emotional experiences are often centered around their own needs and perceptions.

Myth 6: Only successful people can be narcissists.

- **Fact:** Narcissism is not limited to successful individuals. People from all walks of life can exhibit narcissistic traits or have NPD. While some narcissists may achieve success due to their ambition and confidence, others may struggle with personal and professional relationships, leading to difficulties in maintaining stable and fulfilling lives.

Understanding the prevalence and common misconceptions of Narcissistic Personality Disorder is crucial for recognizing the disorder and addressing it effectively. While NPD is relatively uncommon, its impact on relationships and mental health can be significant. Dispelling myths and gaining a clear understanding of the disorder helps in managing interactions with narcissists and supporting those affected by their behavior.

In the following chapters, we will delve deeper into the roots of narcissism, explore its impact on relationships, and provide practical strategies for managing and healing from interactions with narcissists. By building on this foundational knowledge, you will be better equipped

to navigate the complexities of NPD in both personal
and professional contexts.

Chapter 2

The Roots of Narcissism

Psychological Theories and Causes

Narcissistic Personality Disorder (NPD) has been the subject of various psychological theories that seek to explain its origins and development. Understanding these theories helps to uncover the complex interplay of factors that contribute to narcissism.

Psychoanalytic Theories

The psychoanalytic perspective, rooted in the work of Sigmund Freud, suggests that narcissism arises from early developmental experiences. Freud posited that all individuals go through a narcissistic phase during infancy, where they are the center of their own world. For some, this phase is never fully resolved, leading to adult narcissism.

- **Freud's Theory**: Freud described primary and secondary narcissism. Primary narcissism is a normal stage of development, while secondary narcissism occurs when individuals redirect their libido (self-love) from others back onto themselves as a defense mechanism.

- **Object Relations Theory**: This theory, developed by Melanie Klein and others, suggests that narcissism stems from early disruptions in the relationships between infants and their primary caregivers. These disruptions can lead to difficulties in forming a coherent self-identity and stable relationships.
- **Self Psychology**: Heinz Kohut's self psychology emphasizes the role of empathic failures by caregivers. When caregivers fail to mirror the child's needs and provide appropriate admiration, the child may develop a fragile self-esteem, compensating with grandiosity and a need for constant validation.

Behavioral Theories

Behavioral theories focus on the learned behaviors and environmental factors that contribute to narcissism. These theories emphasize the role of reinforcement and modeling in the development of narcissistic traits.

- **Reinforcement and Reward**: Narcissistic behaviors may be reinforced by caregivers who excessively praise or reward certain behaviors, leading the child to associate self-worth with external validation and achievements.

- **Modeling**: Children may learn narcissistic behaviors by observing and imitating narcissistic parents or role models. If these behaviors are seen as effective or rewarding, they are more likely to be adopted.
- **Conditioning**: Inconsistent or conditional love from caregivers can lead children to believe that they must achieve or behave in certain ways to earn love and approval, fostering narcissistic traits.

Cognitive Theories

Cognitive theories examine the role of thought patterns and beliefs in the development of narcissism. These theories suggest that maladaptive cognitive processes contribute to the narcissistic personality.

- **Cognitive Distortions**: Narcissists may develop distorted thinking patterns, such as overestimating their abilities and underestimating others, which reinforce their sense of superiority.
- **Self-Schema**: A narcissist's self-schema, or the framework through which they view themselves and the world, is often skewed towards grandiosity. They may have an inflated self-concept and believe they are entitled to special treatment.

- **Core Beliefs**: Underlying core beliefs about oneself and others play a crucial role. Narcissists often hold the core belief that they are inherently superior and deserving of admiration, which drives their behavior.

Childhood Influences and Family Dynamics

Early life experiences and family dynamics are critical in shaping the development of narcissistic traits. Several key factors during childhood can contribute to the emergence of NPD.

Parental Influence

- **Overvaluation**: Parents who excessively praise and idealize their child may instill a sense of superiority and entitlement. This overvaluation can lead to an inflated self-image and an expectation of constant admiration.
- **Lack of Empathy**: Children of parents who fail to show empathy and emotional attunement may struggle to develop their own capacity for empathy. This emotional neglect can result in a lack of concern for others' feelings and needs.
- **Inconsistent Parenting**: Inconsistent or erratic parenting, where love and approval are

conditional and unpredictable, can lead to a fragile self-esteem. Children may develop narcissistic traits as a defense mechanism to cope with the uncertainty and to seek validation.

- **Parental Narcissism**: Having a narcissistic parent can serve as a model for narcissistic behaviors. Children may learn to emulate these traits, believing them to be normal or effective ways to interact with others.

Early Life Experiences

- **Trauma and Abuse**: Experiences of trauma, neglect, or abuse can significantly impact a child's development. To cope with feelings of vulnerability and low self-worth, a child may develop narcissistic traits as a protective shield.
- **Peer Interactions**: Early interactions with peers also play a role. Bullying, social rejection, or being excessively admired by peers can influence the development of narcissistic traits.

Family Dynamics

- **Family Roles**: In some families, children may be assigned roles such as the "golden child" or the "scapegoat." The golden child, who is idealized and favored, may develop narcissistic traits, while the scapegoat, who is blamed and marginalized, may also develop these traits as a means of coping.

- **Sibling Rivalry**: Intense sibling rivalry and competition for parental attention and approval can foster narcissistic traits. Children may learn to outshine their siblings to gain recognition and validation.

Genetic and Environmental Factors

The nature vs. nurture debate explores the relative contributions of genetic predisposition and environmental influences in the development of NPD.

Genetic Factors

- **Heritability**: Research suggests that there is a genetic component to NPD. Studies indicate that personality traits associated with narcissism, such as high levels of extraversion and low levels of agreeableness, can be heritable.
- **Genetic Predisposition**: Individuals may inherit a genetic predisposition towards certain personality traits that, when combined with environmental factors, can lead to the development of NPD.

Environmental Factors

- **Early Childhood Environment**: The quality of the early childhood environment, including the presence of nurturing and attuned caregivers, plays a significant role in shaping personality development. Adverse environments, such as those marked by neglect or abuse, can contribute to the emergence of narcissistic traits.
- **Cultural Influences**: Cultural values and norms can impact the expression and prevalence of narcissism. Societies that emphasize individualism, competition, and success may see higher rates of narcissistic traits compared to collectivist cultures that prioritize community and cooperation.
- **Socioeconomic Factors**: Socioeconomic status and related stressors can influence personality development. Children raised in environments with significant financial stress or instability may develop narcissistic traits as a coping mechanism.

The roots of Narcissistic Personality Disorder are multifaceted, involving a complex interplay of psychological, familial, genetic, and environmental factors. Understanding these roots provides valuable insights into the development of narcissism and highlights the importance of early intervention and supportive environments in mitigating the risk of NPD.

In the next chapter, we will delve into the identification of narcissistic behaviors, exploring common traits and behaviors associated with NPD, and examining real-life case studies to illustrate these concepts. By building on the knowledge of the roots of narcissism, we can better recognize and address the manifestations of this disorder in various contexts.

Chapter 3

Identifying Narcissistic Behaviors

Identifying narcissistic behaviors can be challenging, especially since individuals with Narcissistic Personality Disorder (NPD) often possess charming and charismatic traits that can mask their underlying issues. However, recognizing the common traits and behaviors associated with narcissism is crucial for protecting oneself and managing relationships with narcissists effectively. In this chapter, we will explore the key signs and red flags of narcissistic behavior.

Common Traits and Behaviors

Individuals with NPD exhibit a range of traits and behaviors that can help in identifying their condition. These traits often revolve around an inflated sense of self-importance, a deep need for admiration, and a lack of empathy for others.

1. Grandiose Sense of Self-Importance

- **Exaggerated Achievements and Talents:** Narcissists often boast about their accomplishments, sometimes fabricating or exaggerating their successes to impress others.

- **Expecting Special Treatment**: They believe they deserve special treatment and expect others to recognize their superiority, often without any substantial achievements to justify this expectation.
- **Dominance in Conversations**: They frequently dominate conversations, steering the topic back to themselves and their interests, regardless of the context or the other person's needs.

2. Preoccupation with Fantasies

- **Fantasies of Unlimited Success**: They may daydream about achieving immense power, success, beauty, or ideal love, often believing that these fantasies are attainable and inevitable.
- **Unrealistic Goals**: Their goals and ambitions are often unrealistic and grandiose, reflecting their belief that they are destined for greatness.

3. Belief in Being Special and Unique

- **Associating with High-Status Individuals**: They seek out relationships with people they perceive as special or high-status, believing that only such individuals can truly appreciate them.

- **Exclusive Clubs and Groups**: They may join exclusive clubs or groups to reinforce their sense of being unique and superior.

4. Need for Excessive Admiration

- **Seeking Constant Validation**: Narcissists require constant admiration and validation from others, and they may become upset or angry if they don't receive the attention they crave.
- **Flattery and Praise**: They often fish for compliments and surround themselves with people who are willing to flatter and praise them.

5. Sense of Entitlement

- **Unreasonable Expectations**: They have unreasonable expectations of favorable treatment and may become angry or indignant if their demands are not met.
- **Exploiting Others**: They feel entitled to take advantage of others to achieve their own ends, often without guilt or remorse.

6. Interpersonal Exploitativeness

- **Using Others for Personal Gain**: Narcissists frequently exploit others to get what they want, whether it's money, status, or other resources.

- **Lack of Reciprocity**: Their relationships are often one-sided, with little to no consideration for the other person's needs or feelings.

7. Lack of Empathy

- **Inability to Understand Others' Feelings**: They struggle to recognize or identify with the feelings and needs of others, often dismissing or ignoring others' emotional experiences.
- **Insensitive and Cold**: Their interactions can come across as insensitive or cold, particularly in emotionally charged situations.

8. Envy and Belief That Others Are Envious of Them

- **Envious of Others**: Narcissists often feel envious of others who have what they desire, whether it's success, beauty, or relationships.
- **Paranoia About Others' Envy**: They may also believe that others are envious of them, reinforcing their sense of superiority and uniqueness.

9. Arrogant and Haughty Behaviors

- **Condescending Attitudes**: They frequently exhibit condescending attitudes and behaviors, looking down on others and dismissing their contributions or achievements.

- **Sense of Superiority**: Their sense of superiority permeates their interactions, making them appear arrogant and unapproachable.

Identifying Signs and Red Flags

Recognizing these traits and behaviors in individuals can help in identifying narcissism early and taking appropriate steps to protect oneself. Here are some red flags to watch for:

Red Flag 1: Constant Need for Attention and Admiration

- **Behavioral Signs**: They always seek to be the center of attention, often interrupting or overshadowing others to draw focus to themselves.
- **Emotional Manipulation**: They may use flattery, charm, or even pity to elicit admiration and validation from others.

Red Flag 2: Exploitative Relationships

- **Manipulative Tactics**: They use manipulative tactics to get what they want from others, often without regard for the other person's well-being.
- **One-Sided Relationships**: Their relationships are typically one-sided, with the narcissist taking much more than they give.

Red Flag 3: Lack of Genuine Empathy

- **Insensitive Reactions**: They react insensitively to others' emotions, often dismissing or invalidating their feelings.
- **Self-Centeredness**: Their conversations and actions revolve around their own needs and desires, with little to no consideration for others.

Red Flag 4: Unrealistic Expectations and Entitlement

- **Demanding Behavior**: They have high and often unreasonable expectations of how they should be treated, becoming angry or resentful if these expectations are not met.
- **Sense of Deserving**: They believe they deserve special treatment and privileges, regardless of their actual achievements or contributions.

Red Flag 5: Envy and Competitiveness

- **Competitive Nature**: They are highly competitive and envious of others' successes, often seeking to undermine or outdo those they see as rivals.
- **Projecting Envy**: They may accuse others of being envious of them, reflecting their own insecurities and need to feel superior.

Identifying narcissistic behaviors is the first step in managing relationships with individuals who have Narcissistic Personality Disorder. By recognizing the common traits and red flags, you can protect yourself and make informed decisions about how to interact with narcissists. In the following chapters, we will explore the impact of narcissism on relationships and provide practical strategies for dealing with narcissists in both personal and professional settings. Building on this understanding, you will be better equipped to navigate the complexities of interactions with narcissists and maintain your own well-being.

Narcissistic Communication Styles

Narcissists have distinctive communication styles that reflect their self-centered nature and their need for control, admiration, and validation. Understanding these communication styles can help in recognizing and managing interactions with narcissists.

Dominance and Control

- **Interrupting**: Narcissists often interrupt others during conversations to steer the discussion back to themselves or to assert their opinions.
- **Talking Over Others**: They may talk over others, disregarding their input and ensuring their own voice is the loudest and most heard.

- **Monologues**: Instead of engaging in a balanced dialogue, narcissists tend to dominate conversations with lengthy monologues about their own experiences, achievements, and opinions.

Manipulation and Deception

- **Gaslighting**: Narcissists use gaslighting to make others doubt their own perceptions and memories. This manipulation tactic helps them maintain control and avoid accountability.
- **Lies and Exaggerations**: They frequently lie or exaggerate to present themselves in a favorable light or to gain admiration and respect.
- **Playing the Victim**: Narcissists may portray themselves as victims to elicit sympathy and manipulate others into giving them attention and support.

Lack of Empathy

- **Insensitive Remarks**: They often make insensitive remarks that disregard or invalidate others' feelings and experiences.
- **Self-Focus**: Conversations with narcissists are typically centered around their own needs and desires, with little regard for the other person's perspective or emotions.

Arrogance and Condescension

- **Belittling Others**: Narcissists may belittle or demean others to assert their own superiority and boost their self-esteem.
- **Patronizing Tone**: They often adopt a patronizing tone, speaking to others as if they are inferior or less knowledgeable.

Charm and Charisma

- **Flattery and Praise**: Narcissists can be very charming and use flattery to win people over and gain their trust and admiration.
- **Superficial Friendliness**: Their friendliness is often superficial and contingent on others' willingness to serve their needs or provide them with admiration.

Case Studies

Examining real-life examples of narcissistic behavior can provide valuable insights into how these traits manifest in different contexts and the impact they can have on relationships.

Case Study 1: The Charismatic CEO

John is the CEO of a successful tech company. He is known for his charismatic personality and impressive achievements, which have earned him admiration from his employees and peers. However, beneath this facade lies a deeply narcissistic individual.

- **Behavior**: John often takes credit for the work of his employees, dismisses their contributions, and makes decisions unilaterally without consulting his team. He is highly competitive and envious of other successful CEOs, often belittling them to feel superior.
- **Communication Style**: In meetings, John dominates the conversation, frequently interrupting others and steering discussions back to his own ideas and achievements. He uses flattery to win over investors and board members, but his charm quickly fades when things don't go his way.
- **Impact**: John's behavior has created a toxic work environment, leading to high turnover rates and low employee morale. His inability to empathize with his employees and recognize their contributions has stifled innovation and collaboration within the company.

Case Study 2: The Overbearing Parent

Linda is a mother of two who exhibits classic signs of narcissism. She is overly involved in her children's lives, demanding perfection and success at all costs.

- **Behavior**: Linda constantly compares her children to others, emphasizing their shortcomings and pushing them to achieve more. She expects them to fulfill her own unfulfilled ambitions and live up to her high standards.
- **Communication Style**: Linda frequently interrupts her children, dismissing their feelings and perspectives. She uses guilt and manipulation to control their actions, often playing the victim to garner their sympathy and compliance.
- **Impact**: Linda's behavior has led to significant emotional distress for her children. They struggle with low self-esteem, anxiety, and a constant fear of failure. Her lack of empathy and unrealistic expectations have strained their relationship and hindered their emotional development.

Case Study 3: The Charming Partner

Michael is in a relationship with Sarah, who initially fell for his charm and confidence. However, as their relationship progressed, his narcissistic traits became more apparent.

- **Behavior**: Michael is highly critical of Sarah, frequently pointing out her flaws and making her feel inadequate. He expects her to cater to his needs and often disregards her feelings and opinions.
- **Communication Style**: Michael uses gaslighting to manipulate Sarah, making her doubt her own perceptions and feel dependent on him. He alternates between charm and hostility, keeping her off balance and unsure of where she stands.
- **Impact**: Sarah's self-esteem has plummeted, and she feels trapped in the relationship. Michael's manipulation and lack of empathy have eroded her sense of self-worth and made it difficult for her to assert her own needs and boundaries.

In the following chapters, we will explore the impact of narcissism on various types of relationships and provide practical strategies for dealing with narcissists in both personal and professional settings. By building on the knowledge gained in this chapter, you will be better equipped to navigate the complexities of interactions with narcissists and maintain your own well-being.

Chapter 4

Impact of Narcissism on Relationships

Narcissistic Personality Disorder (NPD) can have a profound and often devastating impact on relationships, both personal and professional. In this chapter, we will delve into the effects of narcissism on family, friends, romantic partners, and workplace dynamics. We will also explore the emotional and psychological consequences for those involved with narcissists.

Personal Relationships

Effects on Family

Narcissism can significantly disrupt family dynamics, creating a toxic environment that affects all members. Key issues include:

- **Parental Narcissism**: Parents with NPD often demand perfection from their children, using them to fulfill their own unmet needs for admiration and success. This can lead to:

- o **Emotional Neglect**: Children's emotional needs are often ignored, resulting in feelings of unworthiness and invisibility.
  - o **Conditional Love**: Love and approval are given based on the child's ability to meet the parent's expectations, leading to a constant pursuit of validation.
  - o **Sibling Rivalry**: Favoritism and comparison can foster intense sibling rivalry and resentment.
- **Spousal Relationships**: A narcissistic spouse can create a controlling and manipulative dynamic, characterized by:
  - o **Emotional Abuse**: Constant criticism, belittlement, and manipulation erode the partner's self-esteem.
  - o **Isolation**: The narcissist may isolate their partner from family and friends to maintain control.
  - o **Volatility**: The relationship is often marked by cycles of idealization and devaluation, leading to emotional instability.

Effects on Friends

Friendships with narcissists can be draining and one-sided. Common issues include:

- **Self-Centeredness**: Narcissists dominate conversations and seek attention, leaving little room for mutual support.
- **Exploitation**: Friends may be used for their resources, status, or connections without reciprocation.
- **Lack of Empathy**: Narcissists often show little interest in their friends' needs and problems, leading to feelings of neglect and frustration.

Effects on Romantic Partners

Romantic relationships with narcissists can be particularly challenging and damaging. Key characteristics include:

- **Love Bombing**: At the beginning, narcissists may shower their partners with excessive affection and attention, creating a false sense of intimacy and connection.
- **Control and Manipulation**: Over time, they exert control through manipulation, gaslighting, and emotional abuse.
- **Erosion of Self-Worth**: Constant criticism and devaluation erode the partner's self-esteem and sense of self-worth.
- **Dependency**: The partner may become emotionally dependent on the narcissist, making

it difficult to leave the relationship despite its toxicity.

Professional Relationships

Impact in the Workplace

Narcissism can create a toxic work environment and significantly affect team dynamics and career progression. Key issues include:

- **Micromanagement and Control**: Narcissistic managers often micromanage employees, stifling creativity and autonomy.
- **Credit Stealing**: They take credit for others' work, undermining their colleagues' contributions and achievements.
- **Favoritism and Manipulation**: They may use favoritism and manipulation to maintain power and control within the team.
- **High Turnover Rates**: The toxic environment created by a narcissistic leader can lead to high employee turnover and decreased job satisfaction.

Career Progression

Working with or for a narcissist can hinder career progression in several ways:

- **Sabotage**: Narcissistic colleagues or superiors may sabotage others' efforts to maintain their own status and control.
- **Lack of Recognition**: Employees' contributions may go unrecognized, affecting promotions and career advancement.
- **Stress and Burnout**: The stress and emotional toll of dealing with a narcissist can lead to burnout and decreased productivity.

Emotional and Psychological Consequences

The emotional and psychological impact of being involved with a narcissist can be severe and long-lasting. Common consequences include:

Mental Health Effects

- **Anxiety and Depression**: Constant manipulation, criticism, and emotional abuse can lead to chronic anxiety and depression.
- **Low Self-Esteem**: The narcissist's behavior erodes the victim's self-worth, leading to feelings of inadequacy and low self-esteem.
- **Post-Traumatic Stress Disorder (PTSD)**: The emotional trauma from prolonged exposure to narcissistic abuse can result in PTSD,

characterized by flashbacks, nightmares, and severe anxiety.

Cognitive Effects

- **Cognitive Dissonance**: Victims may experience cognitive dissonance, struggling to reconcile the narcissist's charming facade with their abusive behavior.
- **Gaslighting Effects**: Gaslighting can lead to confusion, self-doubt, and a distorted sense of reality.

Behavioral Effects

- **Avoidance and Isolation**: Victims may withdraw from social interactions and isolate themselves to avoid further harm.
- **Hypervigilance**: Constantly being on edge and alert for signs of manipulation or abuse.

Recovery and Healing

Recovery from the effects of narcissistic abuse requires time, support, and self-care. Key steps include:

- **Therapy and Support Groups**: Professional therapy and support groups can provide validation, understanding, and strategies for healing.

- **Self-Care**: Engaging in self-care activities to rebuild self-esteem and well-being.
- **Setting Boundaries**: Learning to set and enforce healthy boundaries to protect oneself from further harm.

The impact of narcissism on relationships is profound and far-reaching, affecting not only personal and professional dynamics but also the mental and emotional well-being of those involved. Recognizing the signs and understanding the consequences can empower individuals to protect themselves and seek appropriate help.

In the next chapters, we will delve into practical strategies for dealing with narcissists in various contexts. By building on the knowledge gained in this chapter, readers will be better equipped to navigate the complexities of interactions with narcissists and maintain their own well-being.

Chapter 5

Strategies for Dealing with Narcissists in Personal Relationships

Navigating personal relationships with narcissists requires a combination of self-awareness, assertiveness, and strategic action. This chapter provides detailed strategies for setting boundaries and communicating effectively with narcissists to protect your well-being and maintain healthier interactions.

Setting Boundaries

Setting boundaries is crucial when dealing with narcissists. It helps protect your mental and emotional well-being by defining what behavior is acceptable and what is not. Here are some key points on the importance of setting boundaries and techniques to do so effectively.

Importance of Setting Boundaries

- **Self-Protection**: Boundaries protect you from manipulation, emotional abuse, and exploitation.

- **Maintaining Self-Worth**: They reinforce your self-respect and self-worth, reminding you that your needs and feelings matter.
- **Promoting Healthy Interactions**: Clear boundaries can help establish healthier dynamics in your relationship, reducing the likelihood of conflict and abuse.
- **Empowerment**: Setting and enforcing boundaries empowers you to take control of your interactions and assert your rights.

Techniques for Setting Boundaries

1. **Identify Your Limits**

   - **Self-Reflection**: Reflect on your values, needs, and limits. Identify what behaviors you will not tolerate and what is essential for your well-being.
   - **Write It Down**: List your boundaries to clarify your thoughts and prepare yourself for discussions.

2. **Be Clear and Specific**

   - **Explicit Communication**: Clearly communicate your boundaries to the narcissist. Be specific about what behavior is unacceptable and what the consequences will be if boundaries are crossed.

- o **Consistent Messaging**: Ensure your messaging is consistent. Reiterate your boundaries as needed to reinforce their importance.

3. Use "I" Statements

- o **Ownership of Feelings**: Use "I" statements to express how the narcissist's behavior affects you. This reduces the likelihood of them feeling attacked and becoming defensive.
- o **Examples**: "I feel disrespected when you interrupt me. I need you to let me finish speaking."

4. Stay Calm and Assertive

- o **Composure**: Maintain a calm and assertive demeanor when discussing boundaries. Avoid getting emotional or defensive, as this can escalate the situation.
- o **Firmness**: Be firm and assertive in enforcing your boundaries. Consistency is key to making sure they are respected.

5.   **Set Consequences**

- o **Clear Consequences**: Clearly outline the consequences if your boundaries are crossed. Make sure these consequences are reasonable and enforceable.
- o **Follow Through**: Enforce the consequences consistently if the narcissist violates your boundaries. This reinforces the seriousness of your limits.

6.   **Seek Support**

- o **Support Network**: Surround yourself with supportive friends, family, or a therapist who can provide validation and encouragement as you navigate your relationship with a narcissist.
- o **Professional Help**: Consider seeking professional help to develop effective boundary-setting strategies and cope with the emotional impact.

Effective Communication

Effective communication is essential when dealing with narcissists. Assertive communication can help you express your needs and feelings clearly while reducing the risk of escalation and conflict.

Strategies for Assertive Communication

1. **Stay Calm and Composed**

   - **Emotional Regulation**: Practice emotional regulation techniques such as deep breathing or mindfulness to stay calm during interactions with the narcissist.
   - **Pause and Reflect**: Take a moment to pause and reflect before responding to ensure your communication is measured and intentional.

2. **Be Direct and Honest**

   - **Clarity**: Be direct and honest in expressing your thoughts and feelings. Avoid beating around the bush or sugarcoating your message.
   - **Transparency**: Transparency fosters mutual understanding and reduces the potential for misinterpretation or manipulation.

3. **Use "I" Statements**

   - **Personal Responsibility**: Use "I" statements to take responsibility for your feelings and reduce the likelihood of the narcissist feeling attacked.

- o **Examples**: "I feel frustrated when you dismiss my concerns. I need you to listen to me without interrupting."

4. Maintain Eye Contact and Body Language

- o **Confidence**: Maintain eye contact and use confident body language to convey assertiveness and self-assurance.
- o **Nonverbal Cues**: Nonverbal cues such as nodding and open body posture can reinforce your message and show that you are engaged and serious.

5. Avoid Arguing or Defending

- o **De-escalation**: Avoid getting into arguments or defending yourself against baseless accusations. This can escalate the situation and give the narcissist more control.
- o **Stay Focused**: Stay focused on your message and calmly restate your boundaries or needs if the narcissist tries to derail the conversation.

6.   **Set Time Limits**

- ○ **Time Management**: Set time limits for conversations with the narcissist to avoid prolonged interactions that can become draining or unproductive.
- ○ **Exit Strategies**: Have an exit strategy in place if the conversation becomes too heated or unproductive, such as taking a break or ending the discussion.

7.   **Seek Mediation if Necessary**

- ○ **Third-Party Mediation**: In cases where direct communication is ineffective, consider seeking mediation from a neutral third party, such as a therapist or counselor.
- ○ **Structured Communication**: Mediation can provide a structured environment for communication and help facilitate understanding and resolution.

Self-Care and Support

Maintaining personal well-being is crucial when dealing with a narcissist. The emotional toll of such relationships can be significant, making self-care and seeking support essential components of your strategy.

Maintaining Personal Well-Being

1. **Prioritize Self-Care**

   o **Physical Health**: Engage in regular exercise, eat a balanced diet, and get enough sleep to maintain your physical health. Physical well-being can significantly impact your emotional resilience.

   o **Mental Health**: Practice mindfulness, meditation, or yoga to reduce stress and enhance mental clarity. Journaling can also help you process your emotions and experiences.

2. **Engage in Activities You Enjoy**

   o **Hobbies and Interests**: Pursue hobbies and activities that bring you joy and fulfillment. This can help you maintain a sense of self and purpose outside the relationship.

   o **Creative Outlets**: Engage in creative activities like painting, writing, or music to express yourself and relieve stress.

3. **Set Aside Time for Relaxation**

- ○ **Relaxation Techniques**: Incorporate relaxation techniques such as deep breathing exercises, progressive muscle relaxation, or guided imagery into your daily routine.
- ○ **Downtime**: Ensure you have regular downtime to unwind and recharge. This can help prevent burnout and maintain your emotional balance.

4. **Seek Professional Help**

- ○ **Therapists and Counselors**: A therapist or counselor can provide a safe space to discuss your feelings, offer strategies for coping with the narcissist, and help you build emotional resilience.
- ○ **Support Groups**: Join support groups for individuals dealing with narcissistic relationships. Sharing experiences with others who understand can provide validation and encouragement.

Building a Support Network

1. **Confide in Trusted Friends and Family**

- ○ **Open Communication**: Share your experiences with trusted friends and family members who can offer support and understanding.

- **Emotional Support**: Lean on your support network for emotional support during difficult times. They can provide a sense of stability and reassurance.

2. Establish Boundaries with Your Support Network

- **Healthy Boundaries**: While seeking support, ensure that you maintain healthy boundaries with your support network to avoid overburdening them.
- **Reciprocal Relationships**: Foster reciprocal relationships where you also offer support and understanding to your friends and family.

3. Utilize Online Resources

- **Online Communities**: Participate in online forums and communities dedicated to supporting individuals in narcissistic relationships.
- **Educational Resources**: Access online articles, books, and videos to educate yourself about NPD and effective coping strategies.

When to Walk Away

Recognizing when it's time to end a relationship with a narcissist is crucial for your long-term well-being. Sometimes, despite your best efforts, the relationship may be too damaging to continue.

Signs It's Time to End the Relationship

1. **Persistent Emotional and Psychological Harm**

    o **Chronic Stress and Anxiety**: If the relationship consistently causes high levels of stress, anxiety, or depression, it may be time to walk away.

    o **Erosion of Self-Worth**: Continuous manipulation, criticism, and emotional abuse that erode your self-esteem and sense of self-worth are strong indicators that the relationship is harmful.

2. **Lack of Respect for Boundaries**

    o **Boundary Violations**: If the narcissist repeatedly violates your boundaries despite clear communication and consequences, it suggests a lack of respect and willingness to change.

- **Escalation of Manipulative Tactics**: An increase in manipulative behaviors such as gaslighting, lying, or guilt-tripping indicates a toxic dynamic that is unlikely to improve.

3. **Unwillingness to Seek Help or Change**

- **Denial and Blame**: If the narcissist refuses to acknowledge their behavior or consistently blames you for the issues in the relationship, change is unlikely.
- **Resistance to Therapy**: An unwillingness to seek therapy or professional help to address their behavior is a significant red flag.

4. **Impact on Other Relationships and Responsibilities**

- **Isolation**: If the relationship isolates you from other important relationships, such as with friends and family, it is damaging your social support system.
- **Neglect of Responsibilities**: If the relationship causes you to neglect important responsibilities, such as work or personal commitments, it is negatively impacting your life.

Steps to Ending the Relationship

1. **Prepare Emotionally and Practically**

   - **Emotional Readiness**: Ensure you are emotionally ready to end the relationship. Seek support from a therapist or trusted friends to build your confidence.
   - **Practical Preparations**: Make practical preparations such as securing a safe place to stay, gathering important documents, and ensuring financial independence.

2. **Communicate Clearly and Firmly**

   - **Direct Communication**: Communicate your decision to end the relationship clearly and firmly. Avoid lengthy explanations or justifications.
   - **Stay Calm**: Remain calm and composed during the conversation to avoid escalation or manipulation.

3. **Establish No Contact if Necessary**

   - **No Contact Rule**: Implement a no contact rule to prevent further manipulation or attempts to draw you back into the relationship.

- o **Block Communication Channels**: Block the narcissist on all communication channels, including phone, email, and social media, to maintain distance.

4. **Seek Legal Protection if Needed**

- o **Legal Advice**: If the relationship poses a threat to your safety, seek legal advice on obtaining restraining orders or other protective measures.
- o **Documentation**: Document any abusive or threatening behavior to support your case if legal intervention is necessary.

5. **Focus on Healing and Recovery**

- o **Therapeutic Support**: Engage in therapy to process your emotions, rebuild your self-esteem, and develop healthy coping mechanisms.
- o **Rebuild Your Life**: Focus on rebuilding your life by reconnecting with supportive friends and family, pursuing your interests, and setting new goals.

Dealing with narcissists in personal relationships requires a combination of setting boundaries, effective communication, self-care, and support. Recognizing when it's time to walk away is crucial for protecting your well-being and achieving emotional freedom. By implementing the strategies outlined in this chapter, you can navigate these challenging relationships and prioritize your own health and happiness.

In the next chapters, we will explore strategies for dealing with narcissists in professional settings and provide additional tools and techniques for maintaining your mental and emotional health. By building on the knowledge and skills gained in this chapter, you will be better equipped to handle interactions with narcissists and maintain your own well-being.

Chapter 6

Strategies for Dealing with Narcissists in Professional Relationships

Navigating professional relationships with narcissists can be challenging and stressful. This chapter provides practical strategies for managing expectations and resolving conflicts in the workplace to maintain a healthy work environment and protect your career.

Managing Expectations

Understanding and managing your expectations when dealing with narcissistic colleagues or superiors is crucial for maintaining your well-being and professional integrity.

Realistic Expectations in the Workplace

1. **Recognize Narcissistic Traits**

    o **Awareness**: Be aware of common narcissistic traits such as a sense of entitlement, lack of empathy, and a constant need for admiration. Recognizing these traits can help you manage your interactions more effectively.

- o **Predictive Behavior**: Understand that narcissists may prioritize their own needs and agendas, often at the expense of others. This awareness can help you anticipate their behavior and plan accordingly.

2. **Set Realistic Goals**

- o **Adjust Expectations**: Set realistic goals for your interactions with the narcissist. Understand that their behavior is unlikely to change significantly, and focus on what you can control.
- o **Professional Boundaries**: Establish clear professional boundaries. Define what behavior you will tolerate and what is unacceptable in the workplace.

3. **Prioritize Your Responsibilities**

- o **Focus on Your Work**: Concentrate on your tasks and responsibilities. Avoid getting entangled in the narcissist's drama or manipulations.

- ○ **Maintain Professionalism**: Always maintain professionalism in your interactions. Do not let the narcissist's behavior affect your performance or conduct.

4. **Document Interactions**

- ○ **Keep Records**: Document all significant interactions with the narcissist, especially those involving conflicts or unreasonable demands. This documentation can be useful if you need to escalate the issue or seek support from HR.
- ○ **Email Communication**: Use email for important communications to have a written record of requests, responses, and decisions.

Conflict Resolution

Effective conflict resolution techniques are essential when dealing with narcissists in the workplace. These strategies can help you address issues constructively and maintain a positive work environment.

Techniques for Resolving Conflicts

1. **Stay Calm and Objective**

- o **Emotional Regulation**: Practice emotional regulation techniques such as deep breathing or mindfulness to stay calm during conflicts.
- o **Objectivity**: Approach the conflict with a focus on facts and objective observations rather than emotions.

2. **Use Assertive Communication**

- o **Clear and Direct**: Communicate your concerns clearly and directly using "I" statements. For example, "I feel concerned when deadlines are missed because it affects our team's performance."
- o **Firmness**: Be firm and assertive in expressing your needs and boundaries. Avoid being passive or aggressive.

3. **Seek Common Ground**

- o **Collaborative Approach**: Look for areas of common interest or mutual benefit. Propose solutions that address both your needs and the narcissist's desires.
- o **Win-Win Solutions**: Aim for win-win solutions that can satisfy both parties. For example, agreeing on clear deadlines and

responsibilities that benefit the team's performance.

4. **Set Clear Boundaries**

- **Define Limits**: Clearly define what behavior is acceptable and what is not. Communicate these boundaries to the narcissist and consistently enforce them.
- **Consequences**: Establish and communicate consequences for crossing boundaries. For example, "If deadlines are not met, we will need to involve the project manager to address the issue."

5. **Involve a Mediator**

- **Third-Party Mediation**: If direct resolution is not possible, involve a neutral third party such as a supervisor, HR representative, or professional mediator.
- **Structured Meetings**: Hold structured meetings with the mediator to discuss the conflict and potential solutions in a controlled environment.

6. **Focus on Solutions, Not Blame**

- o **Problem-Solving**: Focus on finding solutions rather than assigning blame. This approach can help de-escalate the conflict and encourage collaboration.
- o **Future-Oriented**: Concentrate on what can be done moving forward to prevent similar issues, rather than dwelling on past conflicts.

7. **Protect Your Well-Being**

- o **Seek Support**: Seek support from trusted colleagues, mentors, or a professional counselor to cope with the stress and emotional impact of dealing with a narcissist.
- o **Self-Care**: Engage in self-care activities outside of work to maintain your mental and emotional health.

Building a Support Network

A robust support network is invaluable when dealing with narcissistic individuals in the workplace. Colleagues and mentors can provide guidance, validation, and practical support, helping you navigate the complexities of these challenging interactions.

Seeking Support from Colleagues and Mentors

1.   **Identify Trusted Colleagues**

   o **Observe Behavior**: Look for colleagues who demonstrate empathy, reliability, and professionalism. These individuals are more likely to provide supportive and constructive feedback.
   o **Build Relationships**: Foster relationships with these colleagues through collaboration on projects, casual conversations, and mutual support.

2.   **Communicate Openly**

   o **Share Experiences**: Openly share your experiences and concerns about the narcissist with trusted colleagues. This can provide validation and different perspectives on the situation.
   o **Seek Advice**: Ask for advice on how to handle specific situations. Colleagues who have dealt with similar challenges can offer valuable insights and strategies.

3.   **Utilize Team Dynamics**

   o **Strength in Numbers**: In team settings, align with other team members to ensure a united front. This can reduce the narcissist's ability to manipulate or dominate the group.

- o **Supportive Environment**: Create a supportive work environment where team members feel safe to express their concerns and support each other.

4. **Engage with Mentors**

- o **Choose Wisely**: Select mentors who have experience dealing with difficult personalities and can provide guidance on navigating workplace dynamics.
- o **Regular Check-Ins**: Schedule regular check-ins with your mentor to discuss your progress, challenges, and strategies for dealing with the narcissist.

5. **Participate in Professional Networks**

- o **Join Associations**: Join professional associations or networks related to your field. These can provide additional support, resources, and opportunities for professional development.
- o **Attend Events**: Attend networking events, workshops, and conferences to build a broader support network and gain new insights.

Legal and HR Considerations

Understanding your legal rights and knowing when to involve Human Resources (HR) is crucial when dealing with narcissistic behavior in the workplace. This section provides guidance on navigating these aspects to protect yourself and maintain a safe work environment.

Knowing Your Rights

1. **Familiarize Yourself with Company Policies**

   o **Employee Handbook**: Review your company's employee handbook or code of conduct to understand policies related to workplace behavior, harassment, and conflict resolution.

   o **Zero Tolerance Policies**: Pay attention to policies on harassment, bullying, and discrimination. These policies often provide a framework for addressing narcissistic behavior.

2. **Understand Legal Protections**

   o **Labor Laws**: Familiarize yourself with labor laws and regulations in your region that protect employees from harassment, discrimination, and unfair treatment.

- o **Whistleblower Protections**: Learn about protections for whistleblowers if you need to report unethical or illegal behavior.

3. **Document Incidents**

- o **Detailed Records**: Keep detailed records of all interactions with the narcissist that are problematic. Include dates, times, specific behaviors, and any witnesses present.
- o **Communication Logs**: Save emails, messages, and other communications that illustrate the narcissist's behavior and its impact on your work.

When to Involve HR

1. **Assess the Situation**

- o **Severity and Frequency**: Consider the severity and frequency of the narcissistic behavior. Persistent, harmful behavior that affects your well-being or job performance warrants HR involvement.
- o **Impact on Work**: Evaluate how the behavior impacts your work and the work

environment. If it creates a hostile work environment, it's time to act.

2. **Prepare Your Case**

- o **Documentation**: Gather all documentation of the narcissist's behavior, including records of incidents, communication logs, and any witnesses' statements.
- o **Specific Examples**: Be prepared to provide specific examples of how the behavior violates company policies and affects your work.

3. **Schedule a Meeting with HR**

- o **Formal Complaint**: Schedule a meeting with an HR representative to formally discuss your concerns. Clearly and calmly present your case, focusing on facts and documented incidents.
- o **Request Confidentiality**: Request confidentiality to protect yourself from potential retaliation.

4. **Follow Up**

- o **Monitor Progress**: After reporting to HR, monitor the situation to see if there are improvements or further actions taken by HR.

- o **Document Changes**: Continue documenting any interactions and changes in behavior following your report.

5. **Escalate if Necessary**

    - o **Higher Authorities**: If the situation does not improve or if HR does not take appropriate action, consider escalating the issue to higher authorities within the company.
    - o **External Resources**: In severe cases, seek external resources such as legal advice or contacting regulatory bodies for further support.

Building a support network and understanding legal and HR considerations are vital strategies for dealing with narcissists in professional relationships. By seeking support from colleagues and mentors and knowing your rights, you can better navigate these challenging dynamics and protect your professional well-being.

In the next chapters, we will explore additional tools and techniques for maintaining your mental and emotional health, as well as strategies for dealing with narcissists in various contexts. By building on the knowledge and skills gained in this chapter, you will be better equipped to handle interactions with narcissists and maintain your well-being in both personal and professional settings.

Chapter 7

Healing from Narcissistic Abuse

Healing from narcissistic abuse is a profound journey that involves recognizing the abuse, understanding its impact, and implementing effective strategies for recovery. This chapter provides a comprehensive guide to identifying signs of narcissistic abuse and outlines steps to aid your healing process.

Recognizing Narcissistic Abuse

Narcissistic abuse is often insidious, gradually eroding the victim's sense of self and well-being. Understanding the signs of narcissistic abuse is the first step toward healing.

Identifying Signs of Abuse

1. **Emotional Manipulation**

    o **Gaslighting**: The narcissist distorts reality, making you doubt your perceptions and memories. This leads to confusion, anxiety, and a loss of self-trust.
    o **Blame-Shifting**: The narcissist consistently blames you for problems,

deflecting responsibility and making you feel guilty for their behavior.

2. **Control and Domination**

   o **Isolation**: The narcissist may isolate you from friends, family, and other support systems to increase your dependency on them.
   o **Micromanagement**: They exert excessive control over your actions, decisions, and even thoughts, undermining your autonomy and self-confidence.

3. **Devaluation and Criticism**

   o **Constant Criticism**: Frequent, harsh criticism aimed at your abilities, appearance, or character erodes your self-esteem and confidence.
   o **Public Humiliation**: The narcissist may humiliate or belittle you in front of others to assert dominance and control.

4. **Inconsistent Behavior**

   o **Hot and Cold Treatment**: The narcissist alternates between affection and hostility, creating an emotional rollercoaster that keeps you off balance and dependent.

- **Promises and Letdowns**: They make promises they don't keep, fostering a cycle of hope and disappointment that erodes your trust and stability.

5. Emotional and Psychological Symptoms

- **Anxiety and Depression**: Prolonged exposure to narcissistic abuse can lead to chronic anxiety, depression, and other mental health issues.
- **PTSD Symptoms**: You might experience symptoms of post-traumatic stress disorder (PTSD), such as flashbacks, hypervigilance, and emotional numbness.

6. Physical Symptoms

- **Stress-Related Illnesses**: The chronic stress of narcissistic abuse can manifest in physical ailments such as headaches, gastrointestinal issues, and chronic fatigue.
- **Sleep Disturbances**: Difficulty sleeping or experiencing nightmares can be a result

of the emotional turmoil caused by the abuse.

Steps to Recovery

Healing from narcissistic abuse involves a multi-faceted approach that addresses emotional, psychological, and physical well-being. Here are some effective strategies and techniques to aid your recovery.

Healing Strategies and Techniques

1. **Acknowledging the Abuse**

   o **Accept Reality**: Acknowledge that you were a victim of narcissistic abuse. Recognizing the abuse is essential for moving forward.
   o **Educate Yourself**: Learn about narcissistic abuse and its effects. Understanding the dynamics of abuse can validate your experiences and empower your healing process.

2. **Seeking Professional Help**

   o **Therapists and Counselors**: Engage with a therapist or counselor experienced in trauma and abuse recovery. They can provide personalized guidance and support.

- **Support Groups**: Join support groups for survivors of narcissistic abuse. Sharing your experiences with others who understand can provide validation and solidarity.

3. **Rebuilding Self-Esteem**

- **Positive Affirmations**: Practice positive affirmations to counteract the negative self-talk instilled by the narcissist. Remind yourself of your worth and capabilities.
- **Set Goals**: Set achievable goals to rebuild your confidence. Celebrate small victories and progress.

4. **Establishing Boundaries**

- **Define Limits**: Clearly define your personal boundaries and communicate them assertively. Protect your emotional and physical space.
- **Enforce Boundaries**: Consistently enforce your boundaries. Be prepared to distance yourself from individuals who do not respect them.

5. **Self-Care and Wellness**

- o **Physical Self-Care**: Engage in regular exercise, maintain a balanced diet, and ensure adequate sleep. Physical health supports emotional resilience.
- o **Emotional Self-Care**: Practice mindfulness, meditation, or yoga to reduce stress and enhance emotional well-being. Journaling can help you process your thoughts and emotions.

6. **Reconnecting with Loved Ones**

- o **Rebuild Relationships**: Reconnect with supportive friends and family members. Nurture relationships that provide love, understanding, and stability.
- o **Communicate Openly**: Share your journey and experiences with trusted individuals. Open communication can strengthen your support network.

7. **Developing Coping Strategies**

- o **Mindfulness and Relaxation**: Incorporate mindfulness and relaxation techniques into your daily routine to manage stress and anxiety.

- o **Healthy Outlets**: Find healthy outlets for your emotions, such as creative activities, hobbies, or physical exercise.

8. **Fostering Independence**

   - o **Financial Independence**: Work towards financial independence to reduce any remaining dependency on the narcissist. This can provide a sense of security and empowerment.
   - o **Decision-Making**: Practice making decisions independently. Trust your judgment and intuition as you rebuild your sense of self.

9. **Seeking Justice**

   - o **Legal Action**: In cases of severe abuse, consider seeking legal action to protect yourself and hold the abuser accountable.
   - o **Advocacy**: Advocate for yourself and others who have experienced narcissistic abuse. Sharing your story can raise awareness and contribute to collective healing.

Therapeutic Interventions

Therapy can play a crucial role in the recovery process from narcissistic abuse. Different types of therapy offer various benefits, helping you to process your experiences, heal emotional wounds, and build a healthier sense of self.

Types of Therapy and Their Benefits

1. **Cognitive Behavioral Therapy (CBT)**

   - **Focus**: CBT helps you identify and challenge negative thought patterns and behaviors. It is particularly effective in addressing the distorted thinking that often results from narcissistic abuse.
   - **Benefits**: This therapy can reduce symptoms of anxiety and depression, improve emotional regulation, and increase self-esteem by fostering healthier thinking patterns.

2. **Dialectical Behavior Therapy (DBT)**

   - **Focus**: DBT combines cognitive-behavioral techniques with mindfulness practices. It is designed to help you manage intense emotions and improve relationships.

o **Benefits**: DBT provides skills for emotional regulation, distress tolerance, and effective interpersonal communication, which are essential for recovering from the emotional manipulation experienced in narcissistic abuse.

3. **Eye Movement Desensitization and Reprocessing (EMDR)**

o **Focus**: EMDR is used to process and reduce the distress associated with traumatic memories. It is particularly effective for PTSD symptoms.

o **Benefits**: This therapy can help diminish the emotional impact of traumatic memories, reducing flashbacks and intrusive thoughts related to the abuse.

4. **Psychodynamic Therapy**

o **Focus**: Psychodynamic therapy explores the unconscious processes influencing your behavior and emotions, often stemming from early life experiences.

o **Benefits**: This therapy can provide deep insights into the root causes of your emotional pain, helping you understand

and change long-standing patterns influenced by the narcissistic relationship.

5. **Humanistic Therapy**

   o **Focus**: Humanistic therapy emphasizes personal growth and self-actualization. It focuses on your capacity for self-healing and personal development.
   o **Benefits**: This therapy can enhance self-awareness, self-acceptance, and personal growth, fostering a stronger and more positive sense of self.

6. **Supportive Therapy**

   o **Focus**: Supportive therapy provides emotional support and practical advice in a non-judgmental environment.
   o **Benefits**: This approach can help you feel validated and supported as you navigate the healing process, offering practical tools for managing day-to-day challenges.

7. **Group Therapy**

   o **Focus**: Group therapy involves meeting with others who have experienced similar forms of abuse, facilitated by a trained therapist.

- **Benefits**: Sharing experiences in a group setting can reduce feelings of isolation, provide multiple perspectives, and foster a sense of community and mutual support.

8. **Art Therapy**

   - **Focus**: Art therapy uses creative processes to help express and process emotions.
   - **Benefits**: This therapy can be especially helpful for those who find it difficult to verbalize their feelings, offering a non-verbal outlet for emotional expression and healing.

Building Resilience

Resilience is the ability to bounce back from adversity. Developing emotional strength and resilience is a key part of the healing process after experiencing narcissistic abuse.

Developing Emotional Strength and Resilience

1. **Mindfulness and Meditation**

- o **Mindfulness Practices**: Engage in mindfulness practices such as meditation, deep breathing exercises, and mindful movement (like yoga) to stay present and reduce stress.
- o **Benefits**: These practices can enhance emotional regulation, reduce anxiety, and increase overall well-being.

2. **Positive Relationships**

- o **Supportive Connections**: Surround yourself with supportive, empathetic, and trustworthy individuals who uplift and encourage you.
- o **Benefits**: Positive relationships provide emotional support, reduce feelings of isolation, and foster a sense of belonging and acceptance.

3. **Self-Compassion**

- o **Practice Self-Kindness**: Treat yourself with the same kindness and understanding that you would offer a friend. Acknowledge your pain without judgment.

○ **Benefits**: Self-compassion can reduce negative self-talk, increase self-esteem, and improve emotional well-being.

4. **Physical Health**

○ **Healthy Lifestyle**: Maintain a balanced diet, engage in regular physical activity, and ensure adequate sleep. Physical health is closely linked to emotional resilience.

○ **Benefits**: Good physical health supports emotional stability, reduces stress, and enhances overall quality of life.

5. **Personal Empowerment**

○ **Set Boundaries**: Practice setting and maintaining healthy boundaries in all relationships. This protects your emotional space and prevents further abuse.

○ **Benefits**: Boundaries empower you to take control of your life and interactions, fostering a sense of safety and autonomy.

6. **Growth Mindset**

○ **Embrace Learning**: Adopt a growth mindset by viewing challenges as opportunities for learning and personal growth.

- o **Benefits**: This mindset encourages resilience, adaptability, and a positive outlook on life's difficulties.

7.   **Purpose and Meaning**

- o **Identify Your Values**: Reflect on your core values and what brings you meaning and purpose in life.
- o **Benefits**: Pursuing meaningful activities and goals enhances your sense of purpose and fulfillment, contributing to overall resilience.

8.   **Professional Development**

- o **Skill Building**: Engage in professional development opportunities to build your skills and confidence in your career.
- o **Benefits**: Achieving success in your professional life can boost self-esteem, provide a sense of accomplishment, and reduce dependency on external validation.

Therapeutic interventions and resilience-building strategies are essential components of healing from narcissistic abuse. By engaging in various forms of therapy and focusing on developing emotional strength and resilience, you can reclaim your sense of self, rebuild your life, and move forward with confidence and strength.

In the following chapters, we will explore additional tools and techniques for maintaining your mental and emotional health, as well as strategies for building healthier relationships in the future. By applying the knowledge and skills gained in this chapter, you will be better equipped to handle life's challenges and thrive beyond the shadows of narcissistic abuse.

Chapter 8

Helping Others Understand and Deal with Narcissists

Understanding Narcissistic Personality Disorder (NPD) is not only crucial for those directly affected but also for their loved ones who may struggle to comprehend the complex dynamics at play. Educating and supporting others in dealing with narcissists can foster a more supportive environment for everyone involved. This chapter focuses on strategies for helping loved ones understand NPD and offering guidance on how to effectively deal with narcissists.

Educating Loved Ones

Educating loved ones about NPD involves providing them with accurate information and helping them recognize the signs and impact of narcissistic behavior. By increasing awareness, you can foster empathy and understanding, which are essential for a supportive environment.

Teaching Others About NPD

1. **Sharing Information**

   o **Books and Articles**: Provide loved ones with recommended books, articles, and credible online resources about NPD. Information from reputable sources can help them understand the condition's complexities.

   o **Documentaries and Videos**: Suggest documentaries and videos that explain NPD. Visual media can be particularly effective in conveying the emotional and psychological aspects of narcissistic abuse.

2. **Explaining Key Concepts**

   o **Definition and Characteristics**: Explain what NPD is and describe the clinical criteria and characteristics. Highlight traits such as lack of empathy, need for admiration, and manipulative behavior.

   o **Types of Narcissism**: Discuss the different types of narcissism, such as grandiose and vulnerable narcissism. This helps in understanding the varied presentations of the disorder.

3. **Using Real-Life Examples**

- o **Personal Experiences**: Share your own experiences (if comfortable) to provide concrete examples of how narcissistic behavior manifests. Personal stories can make the information more relatable and impactful.
- o **Case Studies**: Use hypothetical or anonymized case studies to illustrate common scenarios and behaviors associated with narcissists. This helps in recognizing patterns and dynamics.

4. **Clarifying Misconceptions**

- o **Dispelling Myths**: Address common misconceptions about NPD, such as the belief that all narcissists are overtly confident or that they are merely selfish. Clarify the psychological underpinnings of the disorder.
- o **Highlighting the Impact**: Emphasize the significant emotional and psychological impact of narcissistic behavior on victims. This helps loved ones appreciate the seriousness of the issue.

5. **Providing Context**

- o **Psychological Theories**: Offer insights into psychological theories and causes of NPD, such as childhood influences and family dynamics. Understanding the origins of the disorder can foster empathy.
- o **Genetic and Environmental Factors**: Discuss the nature vs. nurture debate in relation to NPD. Explain how both genetic predispositions and environmental factors contribute to the development of narcissistic traits.

6. **Encouraging Empathy**

- o **Perspective-Taking**: Encourage loved ones to put themselves in the shoes of someone affected by narcissistic abuse. This can help them understand the emotional toll and develop empathy.
- o **Active Listening**: Teach the importance of active listening when someone shares their experiences with narcissistic behavior. Validating their feelings and experiences is crucial for support.

Offering Guidance on Dealing with Narcissists

Once loved ones have a foundational understanding of NPD, the next step is to equip them with strategies for effectively dealing with narcissists. This involves setting boundaries, managing expectations, and maintaining personal well-being.

Strategies for Dealing with Narcissists

1. **Setting Boundaries**

   - **Clearly Define Limits**: Help loved ones understand the importance of setting clear and firm boundaries with narcissists. This protects their emotional and physical space.
   - **Communicate Assertively**: Teach assertive communication techniques to express boundaries effectively. Encourage the use of "I" statements to convey feelings and needs without blaming.

2. **Managing Expectations**

   - **Realistic Expectations**: Advise loved ones to have realistic expectations regarding change in the narcissist's behavior. Understand that narcissists are unlikely to change without extensive therapy.

- o **Accepting Limitations**: Emphasize the importance of accepting the limitations of the relationship and focusing on what they can control.

3. **Self-Care and Support**

- o **Prioritize Self-Care**: Encourage loved ones to prioritize their self-care and well-being. This includes engaging in activities that bring joy, practicing mindfulness, and seeking professional help if needed.
- o **Seek Support**: Suggest joining support groups or seeking therapy to navigate the challenges of dealing with a narcissist. Sharing experiences with others in similar situations can provide comfort and insights.

4. **Effective Communication**

- o **Neutral Tone**: Teach loved ones to maintain a neutral and calm tone when interacting with a narcissist. Avoiding emotional reactions can prevent escalation.
- o **Focus on Facts**: Encourage sticking to facts rather than engaging in emotional

arguments. This minimizes opportunities for manipulation.

5. **When to Distance or Cut Ties**

   o **Recognize Toxicity**: Help loved ones recognize when a relationship with a narcissist becomes too toxic or damaging to their well-being.
   o **Plan for Separation**: Provide guidance on planning for separation or reducing contact if necessary. This includes practical steps like creating a safety plan and seeking legal advice if needed.

6. **Support Network**

   o **Build a Support Network**: Encourage loved ones to build a strong support network of friends, family, and professionals who can provide emotional and practical support.
   o **Lean on Trusted Individuals**: Emphasize the importance of leaning on trusted individuals during difficult times. Sharing the burden can lighten the emotional load.

Supporting someone who is in a narcissistic relationship and raising awareness about Narcissistic Personality Disorder (NPD) are vital components in fostering a more understanding and supportive environment. This section provides guidance on how to support individuals in narcissistic relationships and offers strategies for advocating for broader awareness and support.

Supporting Someone in a Narcissistic Relationship

Supporting a person in a narcissistic relationship requires sensitivity, understanding, and practical assistance. Your role is to offer help without pressuring them and to provide a safe space for them to express their feelings and make informed decisions.

Providing Help and Guidance

1. **Listening and Validation**

   - **Active Listening**: Provide a non-judgmental ear. Let them share their experiences and feelings without interrupting or offering unsolicited advice.
   - **Validate Their Feelings**: Acknowledge the emotional pain they are experiencing.

Validate their feelings and experiences to help them feel heard and understood.

2. **Offering Emotional Support**

   o **Be Empathetic**: Show empathy and compassion. Understand that leaving or dealing with a narcissistic relationship can be emotionally taxing and complex.
   o **Encourage Self-Care**: Encourage them to prioritize self-care practices such as mindfulness, exercise, and engaging in activities that bring them joy.

3. **Providing Practical Assistance**

   o **Safety Planning**: If they are considering leaving the relationship, help them develop a safety plan. This includes securing important documents, setting aside financial resources, and identifying safe places to go.
   o **Resource Referrals**: Provide information on resources such as counseling services, support groups, and legal assistance. Offer to help them research and connect with these resources.

4. **Avoiding Judgment and Pressure**

- o **Be Patient**: Understand that leaving a narcissistic relationship can be a lengthy process. Avoid pressuring them to make decisions or take actions before they are ready.
- o **Respect Their Choices**: Respect their decisions and timelines. Support their choices without imposing your own opinions or solutions.

5. **Encouraging Professional Help**

- o **Suggest Therapy**: Encourage them to seek therapy or counseling with a professional experienced in dealing with narcissistic abuse. Offer to help them find a suitable therapist.
- o **Support Their Journey**: Be supportive of their therapeutic journey and provide encouragement as they work through their issues with a professional.

6. **Setting Boundaries**

- o **Protect Yourself**: While supporting someone in a narcissistic relationship, set clear boundaries to protect your own well-being. Avoid becoming overly entangled in their issues.

- ○ **Maintain Balance**: Balance your support with self-care to ensure that you do not become emotionally overwhelmed or drained.

Raising Awareness

Advocating for broader understanding and support of NPD involves increasing public awareness, promoting accurate information, and fostering a supportive community for those affected by narcissistic abuse.

Advocating for Broader Understanding and Support

1. **Educational Initiatives**

   - ○ **Host Workshops and Seminars**: Organize workshops and seminars to educate the public about NPD. Collaborate with mental health professionals to provide accurate information and practical advice.
   - ○ **Develop Informational Materials**: Create brochures, pamphlets, and online resources that provide information about NPD, its impact, and available support options.

2. **Engage with Media**

- **Write Articles and Blog Posts**: Contribute articles or blog posts to raise awareness about narcissistic abuse and its effects. Share your insights and experiences to educate a wider audience.
- **Participate in Interviews**: Engage with media outlets for interviews or podcasts to discuss NPD and advocate for greater awareness and support.

3. **Promote Support Networks**

- **Advocate for Support Groups**: Promote the establishment and accessibility of support groups for survivors of narcissistic abuse. Support and participate in these groups to offer help and gather feedback.
- **Encourage Community Engagement**: Foster community involvement in raising awareness about NPD. Encourage local organizations and support networks to address the issue and provide resources.

4. **Legislative and Policy Advocacy**

- **Support Policy Changes**: Advocate for policies and legislation that address the needs of survivors of narcissistic abuse.

Support initiatives that improve mental health resources and legal protections.

- **Collaborate with Advocacy Groups**: Partner with advocacy groups focused on mental health and domestic abuse to amplify your efforts and create systemic change.

5. **Promote Research and Funding**

- **Support Research Initiatives**: Advocate for research into NPD and its impact. Encourage funding for studies that explore effective treatments and support strategies.
- **Raise Awareness for Funding Needs**: Help raise funds for organizations and research initiatives dedicated to understanding and addressing narcissistic abuse.

6. **Foster Open Conversations**

- **Create Safe Spaces**: Promote open conversations about NPD and narcissistic abuse in various forums, including schools, workplaces, and community centers.

- o **Encourage Empathy and Understanding**: Foster a culture of empathy and understanding by sharing knowledge and personal experiences. Encourage others to listen and learn about the complexities of narcissistic relationships.

Supporting someone in a narcissistic relationship and raising awareness about NPD are critical for fostering a supportive and informed community. By offering compassionate support, providing practical assistance, and advocating for broader understanding and systemic change, you can contribute to the healing and empowerment of those affected by narcissistic abuse.

Conclusion

In concluding this exploration of Narcissistic Personality Disorder (NPD) and its impact on relationships, we revisit the key insights from each chapter and offer final thoughts and encouragement. This journey has provided a comprehensive understanding of NPD, practical strategies for dealing with narcissists, and guidance for healing and supporting others.

Summary of Key Points

1. **Understanding Narcissistic Personality Disorder**
   - **Definition and Characteristics**: We defined NPD, outlining its clinical criteria and the primary traits, including grandiosity, lack of empathy, and manipulation.
   - **Types of Narcissism**: We distinguished between grandiose and vulnerable narcissism, highlighting how these types manifest differently in behavior and relationships.
   - **Prevalence and Misconceptions**: We discussed the prevalence of NPD and dispelled common myths, clarifying that not all narcissists are overtly arrogant and

that NPD is a serious psychological disorder.

2. **The Roots of Narcissism**
   - **Psychological Theories**: We explored various theories on the origins of NPD, including psychoanalytic, behavioral, and cognitive perspectives.
   - **Childhood Influences and Family Dynamics**: We examined how early life experiences and family dynamics contribute to the development of narcissistic traits.
   - **Genetic and Environmental Factors**: We considered the interplay between genetic predispositions and environmental influences in the development of NPD.

3. **Identifying Narcissistic Behaviors**
   - **Common Traits and Behaviors**: We identified key signs and red flags of narcissistic behavior, such as excessive need for admiration and exploitation of others.
   - **Narcissistic Communication Styles**: We analyzed typical communication patterns of narcissists, including manipulative tactics and the use of charm to deceive.

- Case **Studies**: We provided real-life examples to illustrate how narcissistic behavior manifests in various scenarios.

4. **Impact of Narcissism on Relationships**
   - **Personal Relationships**: We discussed the detrimental effects of narcissism on family, friends, and romantic partners, highlighting emotional manipulation and strained dynamics.
   - **Professional Relationships**: We examined the impact of narcissism in the workplace, including challenges in career progression and team dynamics.
   - **Emotional and Psychological Consequences**: We addressed the mental health effects on individuals involved with narcissists, such as anxiety, depression, and diminished self-esteem.

5. **Strategies for Dealing with Narcissists in Personal Relationships**
   - **Setting Boundaries**: We outlined the importance of setting clear and firm boundaries with narcissists to protect personal well-being.
   - **Effective Communication**: We provided strategies for assertive communication, focusing on clarity and firmness to prevent manipulation.

- o **Self-Care and Support**: We emphasized the need for personal self-care and the importance of seeking support from trusted individuals.
  - o **When to Walk Away**: We discussed the signs that indicate when it's necessary to end a relationship and how to plan for a safe separation if needed.

6. **Strategies for Dealing with Narcissists in Professional Relationships**
   - o **Managing Expectations**: We advised on maintaining realistic expectations when dealing with narcissists in the workplace and understanding their limitations.
   - o **Conflict Resolution**: We provided techniques for resolving conflicts with narcissists, emphasizing calm and factual communication.
   - o **Building a Support Network**: We highlighted the importance of seeking support from colleagues and mentors for managing workplace challenges.
   - o **Legal and HR Considerations**: We discussed knowing your rights and involving HR when necessary to address workplace issues involving narcissists.

7. **Healing from Narcissistic Abuse**

- **Recognizing Narcissistic Abuse**: We defined the signs of narcissistic abuse and its impact on mental health.
- **Steps to Recovery**: We outlined strategies for healing, including engaging in therapy and building resilience.
- **Therapeutic Interventions**: We explored different types of therapy and their benefits in addressing the effects of narcissistic abuse.
- **Building Resilience**: We provided strategies for developing emotional strength and resilience, focusing on self-care, positive relationships, and personal growth.

8. **Helping Others Understand and Deal with Narcissists**

- **Educating Loved Ones**: We discussed how to educate others about NPD, using resources and real-life examples to enhance understanding.
- **Supporting Someone in a Narcissistic Relationship**: We provided guidance on offering support, including listening, practical assistance, and respecting their decisions.
- **Raising Awareness**: We outlined strategies for advocating for broader

understanding of NPD, including educational initiatives, media engagement, and policy advocacy.

Final Thoughts

Navigating relationships with individuals who have Narcissistic Personality Disorder can be incredibly challenging, whether in personal or professional contexts. This book has aimed to equip you with the knowledge and tools needed to recognize narcissistic behaviors, understand their roots, and implement effective strategies for managing and healing from these relationships.

Remember, you are not alone in this journey. Many people have successfully navigated the complexities of narcissistic relationships and found healing and empowerment. It's important to prioritize your own well-being and seek support when needed. By applying the insights and strategies discussed in this book, you can build healthier relationships, foster personal growth, and advocate for a greater understanding of NPD.

As you move forward, carry with you the knowledge that your experiences and feelings are valid, and that healing and growth are not only possible but achievable. Continue to seek knowledge, build resilience, and support others who are on their own journeys. Your path to understanding and dealing with narcissism is a significant step towards creating a more empathetic and supportive world.